HALLOWEEN

THE SPOOKY TRUTH

For all those who love Halloween!

SINGING RABBIT BOOKS

First published in the United States of America

Summary: Explore the folklore and myths
behind some of our favorite Halloween customs.

{1. Halloween-Non-Fiction. 2. Stories in Rhyme. 3. Holidays and Celebrations-Non-Fiction.}
Singing Rabbit Books, LLC Paperback ISBN: 978-1-7348293-4-1
Singing Rabbit Books, LLC Hardcover ISBN: 978-1-7348293-6-5

HALLOWEEN

The Spooky Truth

by Heather Ryan

SINGING RABBIT BOOKS

Once a year, on Halloween,
   we do some crazy things;
pumpkin carving, costume choosing,
   saying, "Trick-or-Treat!".

But what is Halloween?
   Who fostered the idea?
When and where was it explained?
   Is any of it clear?

Regardless of an answer,
   we still participate,
unaware the tales of which
   these happenings are based.

In this book of Halloween,
    we'll find some explanations
behind our most beloved acts,
    symbols, and traditions.

Keep in mind these declarations
    aren't completely fact.
These myths were told, not written down;
    the records aren't exact.

There is one truth to Halloween,
    it's changed and will again.
Let's see what things we do today
    and how it all began.

Samhain*,
All Hallows' Eve,
Halloween

*Samh·ain (SOW·in)

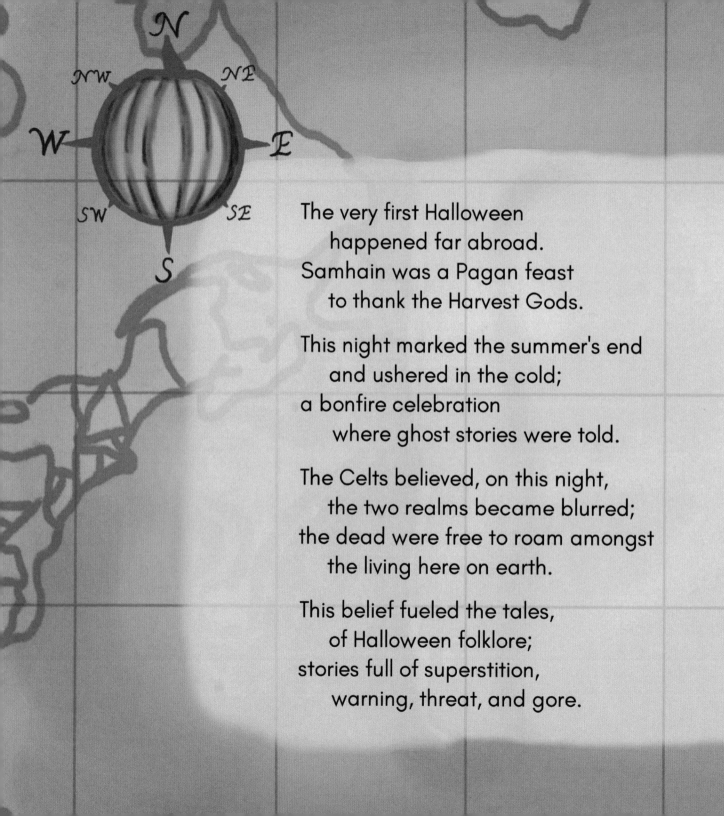

The very first Halloween
　　happened far abroad.
Samhain was a Pagan feast
　　to thank the Harvest Gods.

This night marked the summer's end
　　and ushered in the cold;
a bonfire celebration
　　where ghost stories were told.

The Celts believed, on this night,
　　the two realms became blurred;
the dead were free to roam amongst
　　the living here on earth.

This belief fueled the tales,
　　of Halloween folklore;
stories full of superstition,
　　warning, threat, and gore.

The holiday spread to new lands
  where Pagan views were cursed
but shared the stance the dead could roam,
  October thirty-first.

To embrace the Celts traditions
  and drop the Pagan link,
a Christian name replaced Samhain:
  All Hallows' Eve.

The newly named holiday
  expanded westerly,
undergoing one last change,
  now called Halloween!

Jack O'Lanterns

Carving Jack O'Lanterns,
    most people do not know,
comes from the tale of Stingy Jack,
    a tale of lies and woe.

Jack betrayed the Devil,
    not just once, but twice,
unaware that when he died,
    he'd pay an awful price.

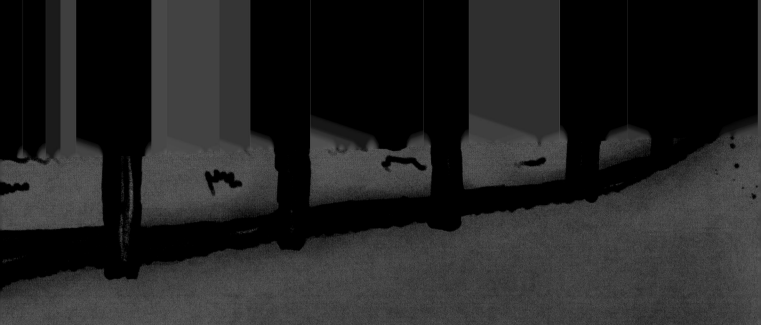

When Jack's life was over,
    on earth his soul was pinned.
For, heaven and the world below
    refused to let him in.

Jack was cursed to roam
    throughout the endless night,
but first was given one small gift...
    a burning coal for light.

Jack carved out a turnip,
    inside the coal was laid.
From this point on, Jack-of-the-Lantern
    was old Jack's new name.

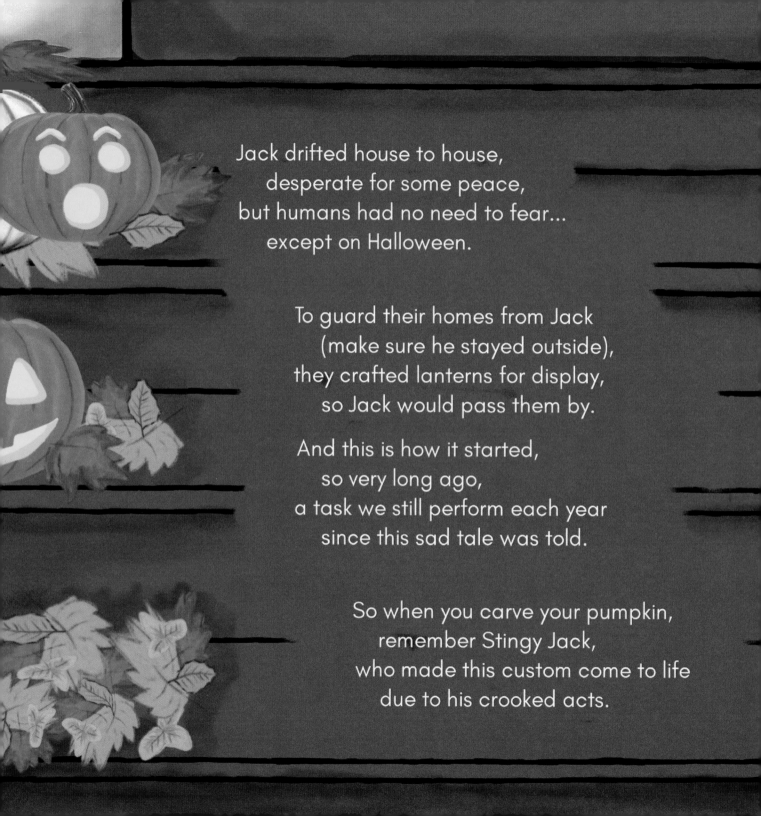

Jack drifted house to house,
    desperate for some peace,
but humans had no need to fear...
    except on Halloween.

To guard their homes from Jack
    (make sure he stayed outside),
they crafted lanterns for display,
    so Jack would pass them by.

And this is how it started,
    so very long ago,
a task we still perform each year
    since this sad tale was told.

So when you carve your pumpkin,
    remember Stingy Jack,
who made this custom come to life
    due to his crooked acts.

Trick

- or -

Treating

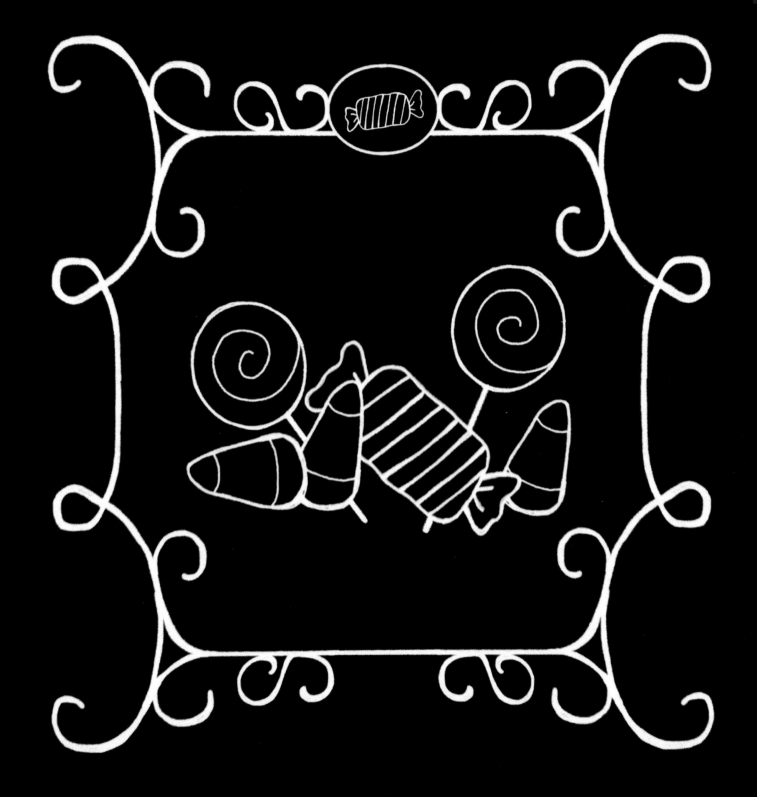

The best tradition of the night
    is going door-to-door,
yelling, "Trick-or-Treat",
    and bagging goodies we adore.

But this is not exactly how
    the custom worked before.

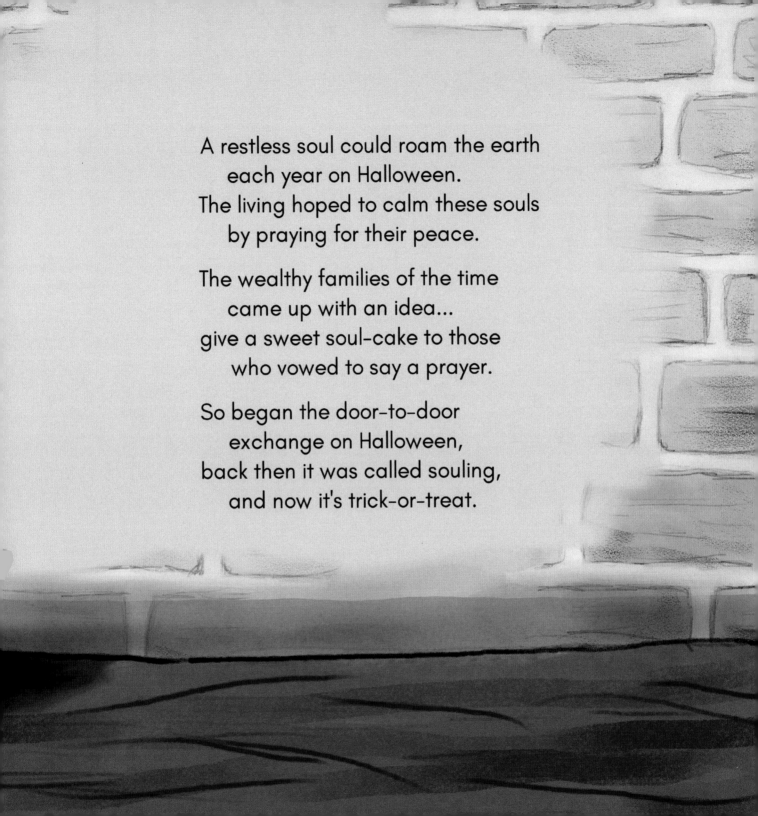

A restless soul could roam the earth
each year on Halloween.
The living hoped to calm these souls
by praying for their peace.

The wealthy families of the time
came up with an idea...
give a sweet soul-cake to those
who vowed to say a prayer.

So began the door-to-door
exchange on Halloween,
back then it was called souling,
and now it's trick-or-treat.

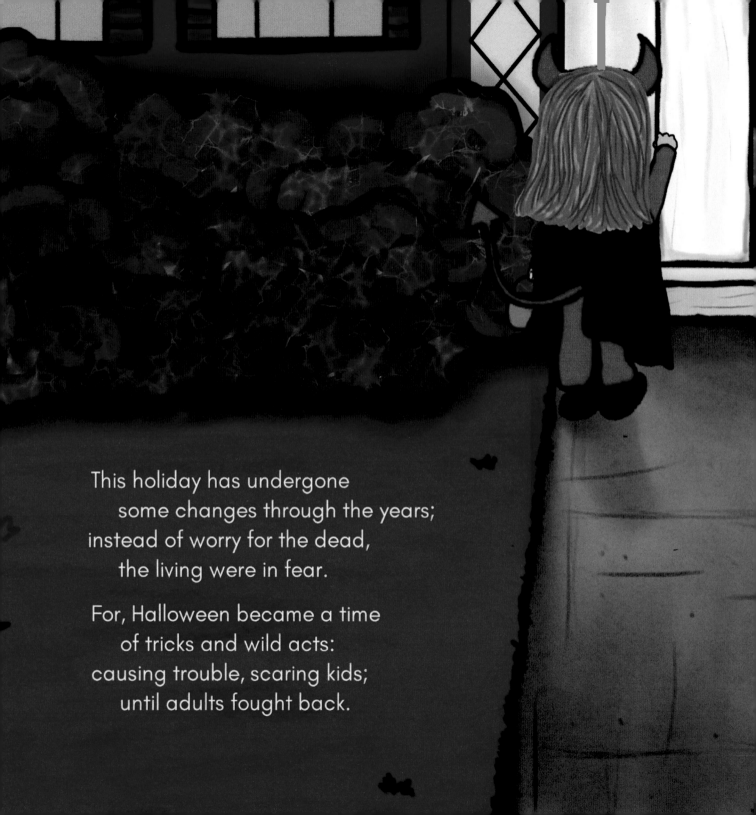

This holiday has undergone
     some changes through the years;
instead of worry for the dead,
     the living were in fear.

For, Halloween became a time
     of tricks and wild acts:
causing trouble, scaring kids;
     until adults fought back.

A plan was hatched and put in place
to quell kids bad rapport...
promise to give out a treat
if one knocks on your door.

The news spread quickly of this deal
and worked just like a charm.
For, kids were busy grabbing treats
instead of causing harm.

Bats,
Spiders,
Black Cats

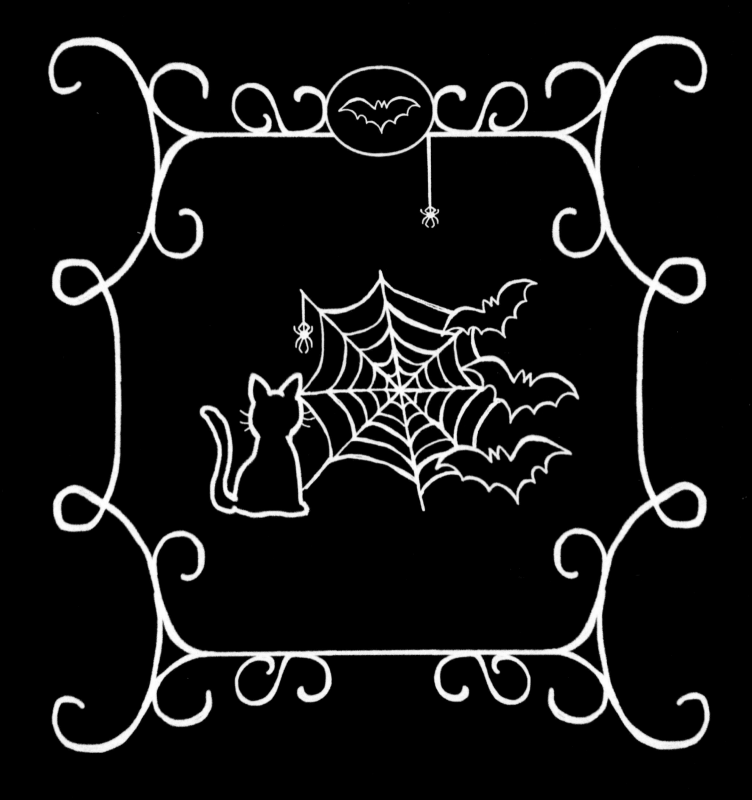

When were bats and spiders first
    linked to Halloween?
Was it through their friend, the witch,
    or by some other means?

Halloween festivities
    took place outside at night.
The townsfolk built a bonfire
    to give off warmth and light.

Many types of critters
    were attracted to the glow,
and soon a host of bugs would loom
    above the flames below.

The bats would flutter to the swarm,
    snatch up the bugs to eat,
and ever since have been assumed,
    as part of Halloween.

Spiders have a more obscure
   connection to this night,
thought to have mystical powers
   for their web and bite.

For how can something so minute
   spin such a pretty trap?
Or cause great harm with one small bite
   without a magic act?

The truth is spiders love to build
   their webs in spooky scenes;
graveyards, dungeons, outdoor spaces
   (sites of Halloween).

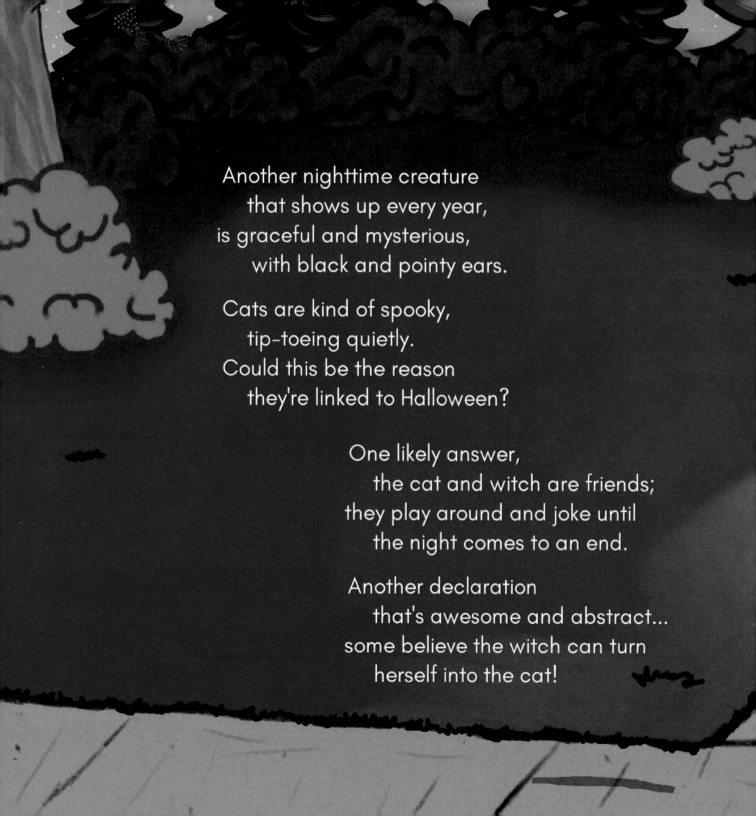

Another nighttime creature
    that shows up every year,
is graceful and mysterious,
    with black and pointy ears.

Cats are kind of spooky,
    tip-toeing quietly.
Could this be the reason
    they're linked to Halloween?

One likely answer,
    the cat and witch are friends;
they play around and joke until
    the night comes to an end.

Another declaration
    that's awesome and abstract...
some believe the witch can turn
    herself into the cat!

Costumes

The living and the dead
are separate...
usually.

With one exception to the rule,
they meet on Halloween.

The dead that roam the earth,
on this hallowed night,
were once believed mischievous,
vengeful, filled with spite.

To fend off evil spirits
while venturing outside,
the living thought up an idea...
put on a grim disguise.

This began the practice
    of costumes on Halloween,
but costumes had a vital job,
    at least, initially.

The outfits had to look
    like witches, ghosts, and ghouls,
so if the living met the dead,
    they couldn't tell who was who!

Although costumes still play
    a part in Halloween,
the task for them to match the dead,
    is no longer a need.

So when you make the choice
    of what you'll be this year,
be glad we wear costumes for fun,
    not as protective gear.

Witches

A group of wise old women,
that understood the need
of finding ways to treat the sick,
examined roots and leaves.

Throughout their exploration
of common garden greens,
many treatments were procured
that offered some relief.

LAVENDER

TURMERI

There were some who didn't like
  these women and their acts.
This group devised an evil plan
  and went on the attack.

They claimed the healing powers that
  these wise old women held,
were conjured from a sinful place,
  a wicked witch's spell.

SAGE

GINGER

RLIC

The rumors grew and spread around
about these healing shrews,
declared to do the Devil's deeds
through spells and magic brews.

Belief the Devil roams the earth
each year on Halloween,
ties the witches to this night,
as helpers to the fiend.

And so the myth continues still,
up to the present time,
of witches mixing up their brews
and casting spells in rhyme.

Although the concept of the witch
was built on wrongful claims,
a Halloween without her there
just wouldn't be the same.

Halloween was first observed
a long, long time ago.
It's altered, changed, and been renamed
since it's first tale was told.

This holiday's ability
to grow and to adapt
is evidenced by characters
who've joined poor Stingy Jack:

a fanged man from Romania,
a monster brought to life,
a clown who made It's home beneath
the streets we walk and ride.

These characters have been consumed
and branded "Halloween";
the subjects come from horror flicks,
novels, and TV.

Despite what has been added,
or how the customs change,
the origin of Halloween
will always stay the same.

So, when the next hundred and one
years have come and gone,
what new additions will there be?
What customs will live on?

The

End

Made in the USA
Monee, IL
10 September 2021

77155791R00026